THE HANG OF IT

The Hang Of It

Brian Waltham

By the same author:

Music for Brass (Peterloo Poets, 1990)
Masterclass (Peterloo Poets, 1994)
The Soldier on the Pier (Peterloo Poets, 2002)

First published in 2011 by Line Press
line@carolinecooper.net

A catalogue record for this book is available from the British Library.
ISBN 978-0-9569112-0-9

Printed in Great Britain by:
4word Ltd Page & Print Production, Unit 15, Baker's Park, Cater Road,
Bristol, Somerset, BS13 7TT.

THANKS

Peterloo Poets published three volumes of Brian Waltham's poems:

Music for Brass, 1990
Masterclass, 1994
The Soldier on the Pier, 2002.

He died in 2002, just after the launch of *The Soldier on the Pier*. He left several hundred unpublished poems, and the present collection is a selection of these.

Michael Cade-Stewart did noble work in sorting out a fairly chaotic archive, and William Wain and I made the initial selection for this volume.

Brian's long-term friend, fellow poet John Mole, made the final selection and offered invaluable help, advice and comments.

Harry Chambers of Peterloo has been consistently helpful with all Brian's writing, and has given valuable advice on this posthumous volume. He has kindly allowed me to copy the Peterloo format.

Another of Brian's friends, artist Elizabeth Stuart-Smith, has done the cover illustrations, as for the previous three volumes.

Warm and grateful thanks to all the above.

Caroline Cooper (Brian's widow)

Entirely

If we could get the hang of it entirely
    It would take too long;
All we know is the splash of words in passing
    And falling twigs of song, ...

Louis MacNeice

Be Wary (epigraph)

Be wary of the old who
With failing sight,
Suddenly see the light.

Be wary of those who,
Free from lust,
Suddenly know what
It is you must.

Be wary of those who,
Shriven and shaken,
Suddenly cannot
Be mistaken.

Be wary of answers
Given by your schools,
But especially be wary
Of dogmatic old fools.

Contents

Early

Ah but there are days that come
Fresh from under stars so close and
Clear that you want to stoop;
Days that hug enough of dew
Never to be knowing and old,
That keep the tang of wet in roots
And wisdom gets no further than
A droplet in a nettle, teaching
The sun about colour.
Then, as morning stays early, there
Can be the very near, catching the
Run of an ant on a wall, or this
Intimate breath of moss or that
Spider tying a can to a tap.
Then, as the roof-tiles prink out
Their wiry lichen, the clouds
Argue about shape and how many
Shadows to let race across the
Hillside maize.
Then, still new, it is old as grass,
Old as the first rain, old as the
First creatures, new as wonder.

Midday

Sun across the landing
And a fly clawing to be out;
Even at midday the top stair
Creaks as if someone
Hesitates, and then the
Stair below creaking and
Down, hesitantly down,
One by one, the
Treads responding.

Nothing is here that was
Not before, but in a
Sunbeam the dust freezes,
The windows stare inwards
And the room, the same room
Is suddenly deep beyond
The living, a vault stopped
By the chill of the dead.

Something was hidden here
That could not be wept out
Beyond the stars and must
Be looked for again and again
Like the one toy that mattered.

Hands

You two, spread out now on my desk very ordinary,
Like the old shoe ad well worn but worn well, veins standing proud,
Blotches and scars that will last me out, a scab from pulling ivy
Off a wall, left thumb a bit gnawed, third finger, not ringed,
Never much good on a cello fingerboard, too much tied
To second and fourth to hit a note and hold it against all comers.

You two, childhood antennae, knowing
Where swelling goodness was, how to centre a nipple,
Teaching me the taste of metal, the smell of uncertainty,
How to eat dust or a wasp, how to ease through railings to
A thirty foot drop or probe the truth of an electric plug.

And even when I knew you better, the two of you,
Still make and break, teaching me blindfold the
Curve of a thigh or strangling the back of a pew,
Good rounded oak tough as the neck of Augustine,
Leaving me to ask questions in an empty church.

Turn you over, you two blind friends, and you're hedgehogs
Suddenly upended before you could clench, but curling now on
Square palms like my father's and lines I don't want to know
Any more than those the Somme stamped on his face.

Enough of that. Let's sort this file, tidy up the desk,
Open an unwelcome letter, dial that number and no
Mucking about, no thumb-picking, no turning over of
That face-down snap you fetched out, no clasping,
No wringing and no more knowing better than me.

Skin

I love what skin does:
Gets a bitten thumb back virgin,
Cleans up a graze, roofs a
Badly squeezed pimple, turfs out
Dirt, holds in blood and lymph,
Signals good and bad, stays,
Until we shrink, a marvellous fit.

I love skin touching skin,
Other skin with its own secrets
And, with love enough, the
Privilege of finding and being found,
Breast outwards, crotch inwards,
Or just nose against nose, all
Primate simple, or my small son's
Fierce kiss or nothing more
Than hand in hand.

Enough

Oh if I could remember all I've heard and read,
Get neurons instantly accurately firing at synapses,
Know that it's all there ready in my head,
Lectures, concerts, endless texts, concise synopses;
How deftly then among foes and friends
I could nudge into a wavering uncertain debate
With 'well no, it's not in D Major that it ends',
Or 'you've got the right battle but not the right date'.
But there would be detail too of lie or fail or cheat.
With the good truth there would come the rotten,
The implacable recall of loss and defeat,
All that I've mercifully forgotten.
I'd better put up with things as they are,
Enough good accessible and the rest kept afar.

More Lost Children

Last night my cane chair faced a high playground:
More lost children than could ever be owned,
Bright toughies, fleeing weepies, the Great Bear
Forever booting little titch over the apex of the barn.

This morning it needs drying with a cloth
Before I sag in and lean, grunting, to find for my
Coffee-mug a level place in the grass. Like a cat
In need of love, the sun nudges my right shoulder.

In the grass among raindrops is a beacon, cold blue,
Signalling that purity is right is right
And that finally I must put aside all that is
Fooling me and is wrongfully right.

But if I move my head so very little to the left,
It is raging orange fire, red-shifted, telling me
Of light-years and bullies long since gone from
Over the barn and that in a millimetre from truth
There is truth about what in an empty cane chair
Can happen overnight.

The Theory Of Everything

"It's everything", he says.

Of course, foremost in maths and graphs,
Physicist, ontologist, entropist, cosmologist,
Knowing all why and what of to be,
Master of the lot, from algae to formulae,
Our Chief of Polymaths, Our Priest-Omnium,
Our Great Man for the Millennium;
If anyone discovered it, we
Knew it would be he.

And we knew he had found it,
That it was enormously exciting,
When he stopped talking, stopped writing,
Went quiet and strange,
Got addicted to lollypops, stayed in bed,
Couldn't have enough of lollypops,
Kept piling lollypops on top of his head,
As if he had gone right out of our range.

We've built a hospital for him alone
With one great room and a score
Of buttons, cameras, dictating machines,
Notepads, laptops, all possible means;
His bed is truly a virtual throne
Just next to the lollypop store,
All waiting hours and days and weeks
For when he speaks.

We know he knows.
Sometimes, wearing a lollypop fez,
He is in the throes
Of beginning to tell us.

"It's everything", he says.

Window

As to this particular one,
I am the world expert.

Its position on the wall, the
Proportion of frame to glass,
The fact that on the left the
Frame is thicker than on the right,
That top left is not a right-angle,
That half-way down on the right the
Joiner left a gap that the painter
Couldn't bridge, that on the left
Anyway the painter slurped a bit
With a small half-moon on the glass.

And yes, the glass:
Apply to me if you want to know
The position of the five wavy flaws
Or the six differently-sized
Spots that the cleaner missed.

As to looking through it
Up or down or right or left,
It's difficult from a bed,
But consult me, if you need to,
On anything to do with one
Particular patch, those special
Square inches of sky that
Come and go and change colour
Without any seeming reason.

Optics

The fly on my window
Knows about God
But not about glass.

God sits in a bowl of light
And must be reached,
But as Einstein found,
On the rim of reality
All paths go round.

Urgent and crass, the fly
Seeks a hole in the universe.
He knows about God
But not about glass.

Across From Here

You winter book with your pin-point
Headings and margins, you balance-sheet
Of hectares, chapter on chapter of what
Is the case in fact, you small print of
Terms, conditions and exceptions,
Black-letter law, girders under the contract.

What do we sign, to what are we bound
Staring at a skyline of each singly punctuated
Tree, gaps where glaciers bullied their way,
Hill that was a lake, farmhouse deep undersea,
His slope ditched away from her poor dowry,
A metre of earth on stone lobsters and shrimps?
What do we ask as you look back with an eye
Empty of pity, you and your flick-knife
Wind and your grey friend, the sky?

Please can we soon be fooled again by
Your chessboard of maize and rape,
While these branches hide their thighs?
Give us now myopia, peering at off-white
Blossom, wondering what its name is.
Leave us to pin back a vine or a bolted
Rose armed for murder or, sloshing in
The ruts, to pick muddy violets.

Hillside Oaks

All that was before you were tall, before
You fought off your treacherous siblings.

Prone here among heat and blackberries,
Siesta for everyone except the ants, I may
Get it wrong, that procession, almost a
Queue down there along the valley floor.

Perhaps, earlier, not valley at all before
The impossible morning. Instead a sea
Beginning to be shore, an emptying
And only after that the careful folding.

For sure there were reindeer and bears
Like ants headed south, anywhere south,
Not planned, not from choice but
Away from deepening lifeless ice.

Round my foot an ant carries a leaf
Ten times its size and there, down there
Is Homo Erectus becoming Habilis in
Shambling tribes headed north and now
In antlike order the left-right Romans
And coming up fast the mob who
Beat them in the end.

Like a tiny yacht, the ant climbs and surfs
With its prize while all else is crusaders,
Streetwise friars, two-way traffic fleeing
War and plague, cannon, muskets, winners
And losers and, like ants who have no siesta,
Those of the wounded who can walk.

All that was before I could lie here drugged
By nothing but air and trying what once
Seemed easy; to be you with no history but
Branches and solve your restless fan-vaulting.

Dark By Five

In the check-out queue
His face is one I know,
But can't put a name to;
Or not here at least where
The smell of new-baked bread
Is suddenly compromised,
Laced with older breath
From sour earth.

What then if he remembers
Me exactly, is eager and interested,
Too much yellow in flesh drawn
Tight to bone, too much knowing
In his eyes, too grateful at meeting,
Too watchful?

When he's gone I'm slow at the
Till, fumble with my wallet as
The cash-girl drums her fingers,
Demand a second bag for the
Carrots, give myself time to be
Longer in here and sniff bread
That is good again and meet none
But strangers out on the pavement.

Getting It Simple

Cold simplifies: cuts down the possible
To white or black, the on or off, the
Snow on a branch or nothing.

These dry leaves, scudding past me
On the pavement, would agree with that,
Although their noise is private.

And it is consistent, but I remember
The kind of mazy sweaty lovely
Doubt that comes with colour.

Like This

To see it like this, and once again for the first time,
Makes me look for a good flat stone to run under,
Rain in the night and now
The City on a lemon sharp October morning,
Rust tang, swearing walls, cold sun on glass,
Such all-at-once clarity in undeniable streets,
With a wind ruffling the bright puddles
And nothing between us and the galaxies.
Small wonder that the hurrying faces say 'emergency'
As they scuttle for stones as big as mine.

Me and Co.

No, the death of a friend
Doesn't 'prostrate', 'desolate'
'Devastate' or any of that
Snow-burying avalanche of verbs.

Morning wants breakfast, the sun
Comes up better than yesterday,
The post is late again and cat is cat
With her own personal problems.

Only that this moon-gear, this
Oxygen-tent, this bubble of world
Is incomplete and that much smaller
For want of someone who should
Be replaceable, but isn't.

Pendente Lite

Do you ever get tired
Of the self you've
Hugged for so long?

Mine was full of a love
That justified everything.

Listen: someone is
Still arguing a case
In an empty court.
Over the years the voice
Has grown shrill
With rightness.

To Both

Forgive him who can't
Stand your understanding,
Wants less of your love
Or only all of it.

Forgive her whom you enclosed
With words, but enclosed you,
Knowing your words, but wants
What you are, or none of you.

The clever two of you, having
Solved the square root of
Minus one and digital pride
And quantum bitterness, try
Counting toes and fingers
And then raindrops and
After that, those stars
You agree are stars.

And if that works, begin on
The very simplest words,
Picking them up like wooden
Blocks, snatching them away,
Kicking at each other's
Wobbly castles, but
Spelling out what you are.

Mid February

What can the old and in their state:
Semen gone, prostate dribbling,
Breathing on half a lung,
Mind heading for confusion, occlusion,
Beset by mental fidgets, seeing,
Hearing, eating with gadgets,
Totter-footed, stranded, clumsy-handed,
What can the old, being old,
Say to the young?

Not much, not much direct,
Not much in words.
But they can celebrate.

But a morning like this they can offer up
Thanks true as a winning team with the cup,
They can count the inches of sun across
A very ordinary wall, or feel at the ends
Of rigid branches that despite and all
There are buds for yet another summer.
They have time, tempted out, to see the
Meaning of detail on the pavement, or
Notice with delight that someone has
Opened a window and is cleaning it.
Quietly they can wish to kick up their heels
At a riot of winter jasmine and that
Here they still are to see it.

Blockage

Those alleys between you now
And you then are ill-swept,
Clogged with discarded luggage,
Garbage from the guilt factory,
Skips full of caution.

It can seem a kind of win,
This dense litter; a backstop
For your getting free.

Only that some traffic, thin
As air, still passes:
The shapeless sidelong,
The stamped untaxable;
Sometimes gifts gone putrid,
Sometimes berries, still rain-wet,
Picked this very morning.

Gulls

Why is that one chimney pot
So special?
Why do the gulls need
Just the one circuit
To scatter the swearing crows?

It's the upbringing:
Street fighting in sea alleys,
Knives out in a wind that
Kicks you under or breaks your
Wing against rock.

Crows boss this block,
But they've had it easy:
Safe beds and below them
Green that stays still.

When the gulls come the crows hear
Chaos, a yell above foam on water
Screaming against the odds and the
Next wave curved for the kill.

Polperro

They always did like tourists.
A lantern on the cliff,
A friendly wave and knives
For those who crawled ashore.

Then the lean years when
They were reduced to the sea.
Boats that went right out of
The harbour, until it silted up.

Now it's back to business.
Pub doorways with port and
Starboard lights, microwave
Rip-off, fibre pasties, the
Old knives whittling at gifties,
Gulls a pound an hour to listen to
And toilets to the left and
Don't leave litter and the
Smell of sewage is free.

Old Shipmates

The blind man and the deaf man,
Sometimes with the idiot, hands
Joined, borrowing from each other,
Almost a complete person shouting,
Swearing, singing, kicking at gates,
Deafening the street.

And me above the din shouting that
They're nothing to do with me and
Lights going on, curtains twitching,
And good friends backing away,
Saying they never heard a thing.

The blind the deaf and the idiot
Wanting to plunge their arms
In treasure or kiss the map or
Touch one single ducat that will
Make them whole.

Shortfall

Brought in from the pavement on Christmas day,
You with your white stick and your dignity
And us offering in our clumsy way
What we didn't want to call charity;
We really did try our best not to know,
Imagined ourselves blind, tried to ignore
Your otherness, tried too hard not to show
Any attempt at levelling a score.
You sat there, maybe trying to unwrap
Your steel-bound packaging of bitterness,
But keeping your hands dead-still in your lap
As if willing them into gentleness.
We promised to invite you here again,
But just haven't seen you around since then.

From The Palace Window

Reading the big cardboard books,
I always found it difficult
That the lovers would grow into
Mummy and Daddy, King and Queen
And get fat and talk of money.

Fumbling a princess in the dark
Always risked more than innocence.
Beyond the door the old fear,
A room of demands simple as love
And tall as wallpaper animals.

And after dragons it
Was hard that my queens
Broke the rule of the story.
Offered gifts which were not allowed,
Spied into my toybox
And would not turn to stone.

Wallpaper

"One more peep from you lot",
Yelled dad, putting out the light,
"And the animals will come
Out of the wallpaper."

And they did.

Fifteen tigers with ABC IS EASY
And holiday snaps pinned on them,
Nine and a half lions and a
Small herd of smudged rhinos,
All of them boss-eyed and all
Wanting to get back into the wall.

The kids used potties to clean up
The droppings, tried to keep the noise down,
Offered illegal crisps and smarties
And began the job of shoving them back in.

The lions went in best.
Seven whole ones and three tails.
Some of the tigers, still boss-eyed,
Would only fit in upside down.

Waiting for dad in the morning,
Are three and a bit smudged rhinos.

To Nico

We can talk more freely when I am dead.

Then first I can say sorry for the huge fact
Of my being there which, as you may
Come to see, is something I couldn't help,
But then sorry again for trying to be teacher,
Too stupid to see that best was to be me
And leave it to you whether that was what
You wanted to be, and worse than these,
A shyness which couldn't say love when
That was what you hungered for, though
Love enough and more was there.

And you, without fear of my outreaching
Interruption, can say you knew all that
From reaching down into damp pillows
And corners of your room where light
Couldn't get, and knew my clever
Stupidity and tried to tell me, tried among
Knowledgeable ice to tell me with what
Could have been a hug.

What do we say meanwhile, you and I,
In the not much time that is left?

Are we still crouched in foreign embassies
Wise in the protocol of what can be said

But is best not to say, can I appear in your
Court or you in mine, dare we break rules
Which have kept empires together, dare we
Say, like small children, what we feel?

May I be young enough to hear and say
All that is simple and direct. May you be
Old enough to do the same.

Failing that, we can talk more freely
When I am dead.

Looking At My Small Son

What ruthlessly you gave,
Please never take back.

But if it's take, then please
At least take everything.
Not just his person, but this
Room, this bed, the car he
Now recklessly screams around in,
Every single loved toy,
Every smallest thing of his.

And be merciful even more:
Take with him all memory,
So that he was what we wanted
And dreamed about, but
Never was.

Grandchild

A bulge only,
But already plotting changes
And for each of us
A newspeak name,
Mine yanks down the sun,
Boots out the afternoon,
Puts me, gummy-eyed,
Continent with effort,
Drivelling on the evening bench.

Soon we'll be simple together,
Learn about milk and fingers,
Be prammed to sleep in the park,
Be washed, coaxed, put to bed,
While you remember what I forget
And we play don't-look, peep-bo
At being born and being dead.

At The Pool

First heart-attack and, floating but ill,
I just have time to wonder about
That latest codicil.

But no, it is a small live thing that bumped
Me from underneath and then, be-goggled,
Said sorry and now, all six years of her,
Sits on the edge and wants to talk.

Without the goggles, hazel eyes and hair
That will slay someone sometime, a body with
Not a millimetre to spare, a way of sizing up
The grandpa me with no doubt and a mouth
That knows what it is talking about.

I've had so many daughters, but not
One of them mine. Then, maybe, I
Would have been so many fathers
Learning to touch but not to touch,
Seeing nothing but what she sees,
Knowing, loving only what she
Already knows she must come to be.

Ivy

Pulling ivy off an oak
Is separating tall lovers.

Or, to be more practical,
A stout hat, a wrench with
Eyes closed against the
Falling nests, mice-bones,
Bird-dirt, sleepy spiders
Tree-dust and general
Sticky mess that lived
Between the two of them.

No question, she loved him,
But did he love her?

If it was love, it was unlike
His roar at a murderous gale, his
Fight under earth against stripling
Princes, his blind wisdom
And his bare winter magnificence.

Keep

You say they built it too well,
That tower armed against all comers.
You say they wanted it perfect,
Those two, and walled themselves in.

Remember, while it stood, your
Jackal envy, you who lack a roof,
It was a high tower:
Stone dressed with a lovely certainty,
Built of all they had.

Preparation

Faces go back earlier to
Get themselves ready.

That morning, the last time
I saw her alive, hers was
A face with the structure of
Those teenage snaps that I
Never believed, but now even
Younger, the cheeks not yet
Ripely full, the eyes not
Yet focused, every inessential
Pared away.

Too early, too late,
For whatever could be said
Between us, but gone back
Through years that were
Years enough and now
Young enough to be ready.

Rock

For Caroline

For all the talk of magic
And once-only music,
I reached your shore
With stuff not fit to land.
The truth is not storms or greatness,
But a hull that would always
Finish in the sand.

Not Odysseus, but a
Bankrupt from rotting quays,
Sewage-silt, sargasso weed,
Come to find your rock and
Yarn about the murderous seas.

Lemnos

You won't believe it,
Nor did we all after all up and down and
Nothing but bawdy songs to keep us going,
But, honest, they were waiting on the quay,
All these gorgeous young birds,
Six of them to every one of us
And us lot all shagged out with rowing.

Well, I tell you, I mean
You know how it usually is
- months to get your hand there,
    then no you mustn't, then alright
    if you promise to be careful -
Well, so help me, with this mob
It was strip off, into the bath, then
Come over here and get me in trouble.
That first night, I don't mind admitting,
I fell asleep on the job.

Another thing,
And you won't believe this either,
But after all that and us all
Getting thin as rakes,
Our wily Jason, him knowing what
It was like, he makes an excuse
For us to scarper, some yarn
About a fleece.

And you know what?
We were all bloody glad
To get back to rowing.

Fancy Dress Party

The rest of us: well you know how
It is, instant recognition, praise
For invention and then, thankfully,
Normal party conversation.

With George it was different;
And, although on hire, he had a
Wicked cutlass and pistols
That really might fire.

He seemed taller and in
Thunder ordered us up the
Rigging and rum of the best
And, in a Ben Gunn tenor,
Started singing Fifteen Men
On A Dead Man's Chest, and
Then, with a knife, threatened
Into silence his normally
Overbearing, faintly contemptuous
And articulate wife.

Pissed, do you think?
Well, no, George doesn't drink,
So it was a puzzle how and why
He went over the brink.

As to what happened after and
More sooner than later was given
The black spot and frogmarched
Back to his schooner, the rest of us
Dared not think.

Exit

That was the day
The love ran out.

We were the same people
Looking at each other
As people do, and nothing
Had happened, but like air
The love ran out.

And it was two others
Shocked at the loss of giving,
Each of us consoling for
The loss of giving.

And it was no use,
All the friendship,
The wise searching
And how and why.
The love had run out.

Boul'Mich.

From this bar where she said yes
I look out at the Notre Dame they
Were building at the time, but
I didn't then notice.

It looks just like the posters, but
I worry about where the loo is and
Whether it's turkish or sit-on, whether
I dare leave my coat on the chair and
Good heavens an Irish pound note in
My wallet and whether to try my teeth
On these nuts and rain that means no
Taxis and a hovering waiter that
We didn't then notice.

I remember too, back through the
Centuries, that having said yes,
She became practical as scaffolding,
Talked of joint income and jobs
And mortgage for a place a bit
Smaller than that, but room enough
For an au pair and nursery bedrooms.

Talking

Still talking, she rang
A week later, really
Nice and well-meaning.

But even if, among
The talking, there had
Been space for talking,
I don't think I would
Quite have managed to say
That although there is
Much good in talking,
Especially when nice
And well-meaning,
Yet there are those
Animal intervals, those
Close-hugged urgent
Illiterate intervals
When the thing is itself,
And that then, then
The talking should not go on
But stop.

I should at least
Have managed a
Kind of sorry that
When the talking
Didn't stop,

But went on instead
Of stopping
And especially when
It went on about
The thing itself,
Then the thing got
Smaller, so small that
It couldn't get bigger,
Even though the talking
Was nice and really
Well-meaning.

Wimbledon and

Forty love........
One moment Mr Becker.
Will the dark-haired girl
In the white blouse and red scarf,
Apparently on her own, second row in
The north stand, four from the end,
Please go urgently to Flat 3A,
Fourteenth floor, Jubilee Tower,
East Bexley, where a viewer who
Has seen her only for a moment
Knows that he would never
Get tired of her face.
Thank you Mr Becker,
Forty love........

Corridor

Miss Forbes,
Remember how often
You have torn them off
At my merest glance
And do not
Walk past like that.
Moaning submission,
Total possession,
Although confined
To bedrooms in my mind,
Demand recognition.
Remember what cannot
Be undone Miss Forbes,
Undone Miss Forbes
And do not
Walk past like that.

Bellydancer

It's difficult to make a woman
Entirely ugly.

They've done it with the face, eyes
Nowhere, lips stretched in an upwards
Rictus, jawbone taut, neck puppet-rigid
And yes, the squirming belly for us
Who have paid our dinars.

But that leaves her bare feet, knowing
They are hers, making love to sawdust,
Speaking her poetry, defying fife and
Drums, however they tire of her
And suddenly change rhythm.

Challenged, they put the next one
In high heels and ducklike,
Off-balance, she grins, rolls hips
And crotch, faces our tables and
Grins always and stamps
Pain up through her spine.

Autorickshaw and Chateau Petrus

Come aboard my hand-painted, my toppling
Dreamcart, my flowered miracle of fifty CC's.
My kickstart splutter, splatter, shatter,
Hold tight while my hawking curdling
Grit-choked first gear racks and threshes
And now at your ease will fly you
Anywhere in Udaipur for ten rupees.

You see now Sir, steering and rearing,
Yes bucking and tossing at the behind of
This lorry which says 'Horn Me Please',
Sideways leap, last-minute now between
Sewage and a holy cow, see too please
As I round this wily squatting beggar who
Would stick out his leg for me to break it
And then ask for money to help him die,
Like they say you have a Petrus wine
That cost five thousand rupees for
Each sip that you buy.

See how she flies, my gilded my
Nearly paid-for fifty CC's, my Formula One
Dodging the impossible in Udaipur,
And here are the steps of your palace,
Thank you Sir, I wish you health
And tonight I too in my smaller palace
Will eat well with my mother, father,

Sons, daughters, sisters, aunts, cousins and
Good heavens anyone else who can
Squeeze in to share my wealth.

Mending a Step at Fatehpur Sikri

A step to this cloister where even shaded
Marble sweats and the ants forget their orders.

Picked out at random, we are street-musicians
Trapped by a score beyond plainchant,
A symposium that will get nowhere.

The beggar, one hand cupped, dribbles at
His flute, curdling the stops, one note up,
One note down.

Black against the glare there are lounging
Cut-outs, and one, stooped down at the step,
Has a hand with a brush in no hurry,
Pausing and, like an archaeologist, dusting
Each rise and fall of stone for when
Concrete might come.

And tourist us squinting out at the board where
Human chessmen waited for the sun to cross
The ruthless grid while Akbar under his awning
Pondered who should win or die, between
Bishop or knight for check.

Maybe, in our key, nothing more can be said,
Except to ask how in this country where nothing
Gets done, these acres of palace did get done,

All in a breakneck fifteen years, but here the
Brush-hand freezes and the beggar on his mat
Is up an octave, squinnying, change-ringing in
His belfry, leaning at the quarter-tones.

Or do they know that their God, like ours,
Makes good jokes? That Akbar, for instance,
Could command clever men, but couldn't
Command the simple stuff called water and
That his dream died of thirst? And then the
Headlong exodus, the packing of curtains, drapes,
The laden elephants, the carts with what jewels
Could be prised out of stone, the courtiers with
Their records, the disgraced astrologer, the
Gorgeous ladies, the women, the lavatory cleaners?

Monkeys at Akbar's Tomb

As if they don't want it seen, their
Masks turned inward on this terrace,
Shivering haunched in family groups,
The young allowed in against the wind,
The old with tails like second-hand rope.

No matter our cousinhood: that in the
Same wind, down by the sewage ditch,
We too crouch and shelter our young;
For we have winter skins, dung and
Matchwood fires, infinite language
And even laughter.

As if they don't want it known that
Earlier than Habilis, Erectus,
Back earlier among the phyla,
Back towards the Cambrian chances
There was a deception, a wrong fork
That led them here.

In needle glances under eyebrows
Across the family or flicked over
Thin shoulders, and now all heads turned,
There is a reckoning, something they
Can't yet formulate, but will when it
Comes, be more terrible than hate.

Railtruck Snapshot

A still-life
In paint that won't dry.

On the half-dark floor
A heap that was a person
And behind it
The outline of a boy.

And still now he
Stares his question
Down the century.

Time begs another chance:
Still now he can walk
In light that he can touch,
And a little love will
Build him cathedrals
To play in.

What would there be of time
That did not have his face
Stamped like a wound across it?

The Hang Of It

You get the hang of infancy
And suddenly it's puberty.

You get the hang of
Girls and bedding
And suddenly you're
In a wedding.

You hock your soul for
This brood of cooling wife,
Listless girl and growing lout
And suddenly the tide's gone out.

You learn to be old, to go
Where you're told, which day
It is, which tablets and on
Which couch you should be lying;
You begin to get the hang
Of that, and suddenly
You're dying.

Ici Cook in Mala Strana

"Say, did Mozart really walk right here where we're standing?"
"Yes Madam, but walk careful. No pavement. Many horse
  and dog and goat and cow. No drain. No toilet."
"But what, if you know, he suddenly needed..."
"He pee at the wall."
"Against that very wall behind you?"
"Yes Madam. Maybe more than pee."
"Against that very wall?"
"Yes, Madam, this one.
"And he really played the piano up there in that room?"
"Yes Madam, but was harpsichore. Then no money and
  They take it away."
"But that's where he wrote all those symphonies and concertos?"
"Excuse me Madam, we are in the way of traffic.
  Ici Cook. Please all follow me."

With A Little Bit Of

The statues and temples put up by Rameses
Leave no doubt that he was great.
Single-handed in his chariot, for instance,
He won Kadesh.

But with all those arrows flying, you might
Think he must have had quite a bit of luck.

The despatches of Caesar are more oblique,
Leaving for you to decide that he was great,

Although, what with two legions lost in
German forests and the ships nearly wrecked
On English beaches, you might think
That he had quite a bit of luck.

That is until, back at Rome,
He ran out of luck.

Then there was Napoleon with all
Those victories under his belt.

Of a young lieutenant, brave and
Able, brought to him for promotion,
He asked:
Does he have luck?

Theatre

It's wasteful, but nowadays
I rarely stay to the end.
The interval sees me at the bar
Watching the others file back in.

It's even worse with dreams.
Whether plot or actors
Or sheer lousy direction,
The first Act has me picking
My thumb and then shoving
Past a scolding row of faces.

Ward 5

They play it to pass the time,
Time long as Sister's cloak, short
As flex on the ceiling light.
The aim is to get to the end and
Everyone joins in and everyone
Gets the same dark prize.

On this white, painkilling cave
They know the rules as well
As stone age man.
Fear is not of void, but of
The next ten minutes.
Being ahead is a falling graph,
Winning is a screen round the bed
And a tired houseman signing
That you're home.

For My Doctors

Bend down very close
And listen for words.
It was often difficult
To get the words out.

Lift my eyelids for
What looks back.
Looking back was often
More than I could manage.

See if my left hand
Is curling for a
Cello fingerboard.
Not expert, but going
Where it once went.

Check whether
The ends of my lips
Are going upwards.

None of these?
Sure?

Oh then switch it off,
Switch me off, go and have
A cup of tea and grumble
About salaries and your
Impossible children.

In Passing

Never listen, you who will be oldies,
If us oldies do not give thanks,
And never ask us to whom we
Should have given them.

Thanks, if we have none of them,
Are end-stops, rust-free memories,
Small revenges locked behind rock
We never did know how to open.

Thanks, if we give them, are not
For us to explain. They are guesses
That with luck enough you will see
The hand of a leaf cupped for its
Trembling cargo of rain.